The Wonderful World of Audiobooks/

Earn Money from Home as an Audiobook Narrator

by Laura Johnson

It was suggested to me by a friend, that I write a book about my experiences as an audiobook narrator and producer. Being fairly new to the profession, I was not sure I had that much to offer. But after posting on some of the group Facebook sites, I am a member of, I discovered that there are a whole group of people out there who are interested in finding out, how to do, what I am now doing. The response to my posting was amazing. I was simply looking for a designer to do my eBook cover. I am still answering responses, after several days. I figured there may be a lot more people out there, that might want to find out how to earn a living, from the comfort of their own home, by learning how to become an audiobook narrator and producer. If you are interested in discovering the wonderful world of audiobooks, as a narrator and producer, this is the book for you. These next few pages will tell you how I discovered a work from home career (not just a job), that is fun, exciting, and fulfilling. So, let's get started!

I was first introduced to the world of audiobook narration and production while searching for a "work at home" job. I had been searching for a "work at home" job, since I first retired. Let's see, that is approximately, seven years ago. Yeah, you read that right, seven years. Now, not to say I searched every single day for seven years. I might go months without looking, but then one day I would get bored or need some extra cash and start searching again. But sooner or later, I would get involved with something else, and on the back burner, the job search would go.

I wasn't really sure what type of job I was looking for. I just knew I wanted a job that I could do at home. I wanted to work my own hours and only three or four days a week, if possible. In other words, I wanted a very flexible schedule. And if I wanted to sleep late, I could. Or maybe, I wanted to work late nights or very early mornings. Whatever, the days or hours I would put in, I wanted them to be my choice. For years, I worked the days and hours someone else wanted, so, I kept searching and searching, but just never seemed to find the right job. During the first year of my retirement, I decided to work for Kelly Services. At least there was some flexibility with their company. I could accept an assignment or turn it down. I did a good bit of Mystery Shopping for Kelly Services, but I actually had to leave home, and go to a retail store or a financial institution. Still it was different, interesting, and fun. But, it still was not what I was looking for.

A little over a year ago, I moved to New Jersey from Florida, to help my, now single son, take care of his four children, ages five to thirteen. Even though this was a huge step for me, I didn't hesitate. My family needed me. My retirement life was pretty cool. I was secretary of a non-profit organization. I lived in a beautiful Senior complex, that, I thought, was nicer than a Hilton. I lived on the Treasure Coast of Florida, in Vero Beach. I had a bevy of friends, and I sang in the church choir. But all that didn't matter, because my son and his children needed me. When it comes to my family, I will always be there for them.

Besides caring for the children while my son works, I also began to Homeschool them. Wow! That is a job in itself, unpaid of course, but one I dearly love. It is so wonderful to watch these children as they travel down this path of discovering and learning new things. And all in the safety of their own home.

Being a family of six, money is tight, so I took up the "work at home" job search, again. I found an ad on Craig's List that lead to online Mystery Shopping. Now this I could do. I loved Mystery Shopping through Kelly Services. Well, I had a chance to do it from home, and on-line. I soon discovered, it was not much fun, and it was very low pay. I would have to make about twenty-five to thirty calls a week from a spreadsheet that I had to download. I had to pretend to be a home owner, looking for a new car, need life insurance, want debt relief, want to go back and get a degree, and a host of other things. After faking all of these scenarios, I had to answer my phone constantly from numerous businesses trying to sell me, what I said, I needed. My phone rang non-stop for days on end. I had to take screen shots of all the websites I visited and information I filled out. All of this work, and I only made, $1.00 per call, $1.00 per screen shot, etc. It was not worth it. And on top of that, I waited until the end of the month to get paid. Needless to say, that job didn't last long, maybe a month. After that fiasco, I found a telemarketing job on Craig's List with a local company. It lasted about 2 months. It was very low pay and more time than I wanted to spend calling businesses with a rehearsed script. So, I started looking for something else, again.

I joined a couple of "work at home" Facebook groups, signed up for "work at home" newsletters from blogs I had read on the Internet, and even attended a week long free Webinar for those interested in "working at home". The guest speakers on the Webinar, were Entrepreneurs from all walks of life and all types of businesses. They all offered you something free, if you signed up for the Webinar. Anything from an eBook to another free Webinar, and all were wanting to sign you up for their "paying course" so you could learn how to make money, you guessed it, "working at home". Now, don't get me wrong, I don't begrudge these people their right to earn a living, but I wanted a way to "make" money, not "spend" money.

A couple of months ago, I ran across an interesting ad on one of the blog sites, I was reading. It simply said,

"FREE 5-DAY AUDIOBOOK AUDITION CHALLENGE" and the instructor of the course was Krystal Wascher. Well, it was "FREE" and it was a 'CHALLENGE". I love "A CHALLENGE" and who doesn't love "FREE"? The ad further read: Get five days of in-depth online video training and action steps! Here's what you'll learn!

- How to download and use the free audio recording program, Audacity.

- How to write an appealing ACX narrator profile (even if you're just getting started.)
- Audio sample selection and recording.
- Where to find books to audition for.
- How to choose the books for your voice and interests.
- Prepare and submit a real audition!

I thought, WOW! I could actually learn how to become an audiobook narrator in five days, for free! This sounded so exciting. I love reading and I could learn to share that love, with others, through audiobooks, and actually get paid doing it. So, I clicked the "Take the Challenge" button. Krystal Wascher, and her course, changed my life and opened up the wonderful world of audiobook narration and production.

I'd like to tell you a little about Krystal Wascher, especially, since she is the person who literally changed my life. Krystal is an audiobook producer, narrator, author, licensed attorney, and the founder of *Audiobook School*. *Audiobook School* is an online learning center that teaches aspiring audiobook narrators, authors, and bloggers how to create high quality audiobooks.

Krystal is also the creator of *Audiobooks with Audacity* and the author of *Narration: A Beginners Guide to Creating Audiobooks for Audible and iTunes*. Krystal also offers narration and voice over services. You can visit her website at https://krystalwascher.com to read about all the amazing services Krystal Wascher provides.

Besides all of her accomplishments, I can attest to the fact that Krystal Wascher is an excellent course instructor. All three of her courses that I took, *5-Day Audiobook Audition Challenge*, *Audiobooks 101*, and *Audiobooks with Audacity* were so very easy to follow and understand. On the videos, she went through every lesson, step by step, explaining it so that even someone, like me, who is not technically savvy, could comprehend what was being taught.

Once I started the audition challenge course, I was definitely excited, but also a little apprehensive. Most of the curriculum looked easy to learn. The course started out with the Orientation video. Then, Day 1 was "Warming Up to the Mic", which also included downloading the Audacity software. Day 2 video was "Getting Started on ACX", which included creating an account and setting up a profile. Then I saw, Day 3… Step 3… "Recording and Editing" tutorial. Recording, no problem. I had been an entertainer for over 30 years and knew my way around a microphone. But editing? No way could I wrap my non-technical brain around actually editing something on a recorded track. Well, I am living, breathing, proof that if you set your mind to something you have a fierce desire to do, and you follow step by step instructions, you can do it! Day 4 video was "Book Search". That was picking titles to record as samples. And Day 5, was AUDITION DAY. It was finally here. A little note here, just so you know, I did not actually submit an audition on Day 5. I was too scared and nervous. Yes, I had uploaded samples to my profile, but I just couldn't bring myself to submit an audition yet. That does not mean you won't be able to. The good thing is that everyone can learn and work at their own pace. Krystal gives the materials to work with, it's up to you how you utilize what she gives you.

I had no clue what I was doing in the beginning, but with the free software, Audacity, and Krystal's excellent step by step instructions, I not only was able to record, but, eventually, also edit and master my own recordings. If I can do this at 69 years old, with no technical savvy, you can do it too. I am here to tell you that the course was enlightening, fun, and easy to understand. When I was finished with the course, I had a profile on ACX, as well as, two samples of my recorded narrations, even though I had not yet, submitted an actual audition.

Of course, Krystal does not just leave you hanging. She is very supportive and responds to any questions you might have. I simply send her an email and she will answer back within a day or two. I took her course back in April and I still ask her questions or just send her an update as to how I am progressing. She always answers me back.

Shortly after finishing the *5-Day Audiobook Audition Challenge*, I enrolled in her full course, *Audiobooks 101*. I wanted more knowledge. As much as I could soak up. I wanted to feel more confident. I researched other courses, checked out Facebook Audiobook groups, blogs about audiobooks, and anything I could find about the world of audiobook narration. In my opinion, Krystal Wascher had the best course, especially for someone like me, who was a total novice in every aspect of the profession.

The *Audiobooks 101* course was everything the 5-Day course was, but more in depth. There are 5 Modules. Module 1 is "The Big Business of Audiobooks". Module 2 is "What's Involved". Module 3 is "Money Talks". Module 4 is "Gear and Studio Set Up". Module 5 is "Finding Work as a Narrator". All modules are chock full of invaluable information about the world of audiobooks and well worth the time and money. But, I will add here, you do not have to take this course to be a successful narrator.

I wanted to absorb as much information as I could. You can never learn too much. The more knowledge you have about your profession, I believe, the better job you can do.

So, I started on the *Audiobooks 101* course. And you know what happened? Before I was even halfway through the course, I received my first offer to narrate and produce an audiobook! Wow! What an awesome feeling. And, naturally, the doubts started setting in. Am I ready for this? Am I good enough? Can I really record and master an entire audiobook? I quickly emailed Krystal and she put all my fears to rest and was very supportive and encouraging. So, I went to work. I actually finished that audiobook within a couple of weeks. It went on sale on Amazon, Audible.com., and iTunes on May 3. My second audiobook went on sale May 23. My third audiobook has been approved by the Rights Holder and is awaiting approval from the ACX Quality Assurance Team. The ACX Quality Assurance Team makes sure that all titles adhere to and meet ACX Audio submission Requirements, in order to help ensure customers get a great overall listening experience, therefore, maximizing sales potential. I just received and accepted an offer to do my fourth audiobook. All of this happened within a couple of months.

Now, I am not saying or promising that you will have the same results, but it could happen. You could even do better. But nothing will happen, if you don't take that first step. If you truly think, being an audiobook narrator and producer is something you would enjoy, then go for it!

There is a third course you should know about. It is Krystal's *Audiobooks with Audacity.* This is a 15 Module intense study about working with audiobooks. Module 1 is about audiobooks industry basics. Module 2 has options for working with audiobooks. Module 3 covers finding work. Module 4 discusses money and payments. Module 5 is working through ACX. Module 6 is working through Author's Republic. Module 7 explains ACX rules. Module 8 is all about recording space and equipment. Module 9 is getting started with Audacity. Module 10 is Manuscript prep and voice development. Module 11 is recording techniques and tutorials. Module 12 delves more extensively into audiobook editing. Module 13 is proofing. Module 14 covers sound mastery basics. Module 15 gives you the final steps. At the end of the course is a question and answer section and of course a help section. Krystal is always available to help you in any way she can.

By now you are probably curious about ACX. What is ACX? ACX stands for *Audiobook Creation Exchange*. It is a marketplace where authors, literary agents, publishers, and other Rights Holders can connect with narrators, engineers, recording studios, and other producers capable of producing a finished audiobook. The result is that more audiobooks will be made.

When you join ACX, for free, you set up a profile. It's really a very simple process. You basically fill in the blanks, add a profile picture, upload your voice samples, and designate how you prefer to be paid. Krystal walks you through all of this in her Audiobook courses. ACX also walks you through the entire process. I like the designation of how I want to be paid. You, as a narrator/producer can be paid by "Royalty Share" or PFH (per finished hour). Krystal goes over both of these in detail in her audiobook courses. You are able to edit your profile anytime you choose. You can also delete samples and add new ones.

After setting up your profile, you continue on to fill in your account information. Here is where you enter personal information: Name, Address, Company (if applicable), Email, and Contact phone number. Next, you provide tax information that will be submitted and verified by the IRS. Your bank information is added so you can receive Royalty checks from ACX. PFH payments are paid directly to you by the Rights Holder, usually through PayPal. As a little explanation, PFH is the actual length of the finished book. It is not the extra time put into editing and mastering. It is the actual reading time of the audiobook. Sounds a little iffy, but all of this is explained during Krystal's courses. And you set your own PFH rate, not the rights holder. You will learn how to figure out what rate to set during any one Krystal's courses. As a member of ACX you are protected in all of your transactions.

The ACX website is chock full of valuable information that you can use to further your career as a narrator and producer. You can read about ACX and how it works at https://www.acx.com/ . You have access to Educational Resources such as, ACX University, How to Promote Yourself, numerous and various Video Lessons and Resources. As I said before, all of this is free to you. There is even an ACX Blog to which you can subscribe and hear from other authors and narrators, like yourself.

I have researched other similar sites and checked out Facebook groups and blogs about audiobook recording. The general consensus is that ACX is a cut above the rest.

I love being able to search for Titles that need narrators. At any given time, there are almost 3000 titles in need of narrators. I can audition for any of those titles. Sometimes, I might have three to five auditions pending at the same time. Am I selected for all of them? Of course not. Do I get offended if I am not chosen? Heck no. Authors are looking for a certain type of voice and they know the sound they want when they hear it. Do not ever take rejections personally. Your voice will not be the right voice for every book you audition for. Accept the rejection gracefully and move on to the next audition. I certainly have had more rejections, than offers, but I don't let it get to me. It is a part of the business. Besides, I would never have time to produce all the titles I audition for. I like to have several auditions pending at all times, because it is nice to be able to pick and choose. I am thankful for the offers I have received and the audiobooks, I have recorded and produced. And there will always be another offer, just around the corner. Oh, and by the way, just because you receive an offer does not mean you have to accept it. An offer is just that, an offer. You can negotiate with the Rights Holder. If you both agree on the price and time frame, awesome, but if you cannot agree, then do not accept the offer.

On my second book, I hesitated to continue because after receiving and reading the manuscript, there were too many errors. It needed another edit pass. So, I contacted the Rights Holder. They edited the book for a second time and returned a much cleaner manuscript. Everyone was happy, and the customer will have a much better listening experience. I have received two offers on two audiobooks that I never even auditioned for, so having good samples on your profile pays off. ACX has a lot to offer you. Just take advantage of it and use the resources available. And if you need help, ACX techs are just a phone call away.

One very important thing you should know is your upfront investment. Here it comes, right? What is it going to cost me? Well, it doesn't cost as much as you might think to become an audiobook narrator. It is not expensive to get started. The *5-Day Audiobook Audition Challenge Course* was free. After I finished the course, I bought a microphone, an Audio-technica cardioid dynamic, USB/XLR. I found it, brand new, on Amazon, and on sale, for only $62.00. I love it and the sound is great. I already had a set of headphones, but you can get those for $25 or less on Amazon. Walmart even has good headphones for $10. A side note. I got my first offer, when the Rights Holder heard one of my samples on my profile. Those had been recorded through the headset microphone, before I bought my current microphone. Go figure. I have since redone those recordings and the samples have all now been recorded with my new microphone.

As for recording space, I record at my desk, in a corner of my living room, on my HP desktop computer. Some narrators even record in a closet. And a desktop is not necessary. Many narrators use a laptop. Point being, you do not have to spend big bucks to buy expensive equipment or to set up a fancy recording studio. As far as privacy, hopefully, you have a supportive family. My family is very supportive and gives me quiet time while I am recording. Even the five and seven-year-old grandkids know to be quiet while Grandma is recording.

OK, I have told you a little about how I got started in my audiobook narration career. I have told you a little about Krystal Wascher and her accomplishments. I, also, told you a little about ACX, the exchange I work through to find the audiobooks to record and produce. Now, I think you should know a little about the authors you will be working with.

ACX makes it fairly easy for authors to search for narrators for their titles to be turned into audiobooks. They also make it easy for narrators to search for titles to submit auditions for. Once you log onto ACX, there is a search engine. You can search for "producers for hire', (that's what the author searches), or "titles accepting auditions" (that's what you search). Once an author posts the information about their book, they simply wait for the auditions to start coming in. You, as a narrator, will search through the "titles accepting auditions", until you find one or more that interest you enough to prepare an audition to submit. Please, don't worry, I know I said earlier that there are almost 3000 titles at any given time. You do not have to search through all of those titles. When you set up your account with ACX, there will be a section where you will set up *Profile* filters and *Titles* filters. Under *Profile* filters, you will list *gender, genre, and project rate.* If you are female, you probably will want to stick with titles looking for female *narrators.* Sometimes the gender will suggest male or female narrators. *Genre* is the type book you would enjoy narrating, such as Romance, Science Fiction, Thriller, etc. And of course, *Project Rate* is the type of pay you will accept, Royalty Share, or PFH, or both. *Titles* filters include: Fiction/Non-Fiction, Language, Accent, Voice Age, Vocal Style, and Project length. So, you see, you can filter the title choices down considerably to only those you are comfortable doing. Once you submit your audition, you sit back, relax, and wait for the email notification from

ACX that says "Congratulations, You Have an Offer".

Alright, here is the fun part. You are going to actually narrate and produce an audiobook. Now, please don't react like I did in the beginning. I was so intimidated by the thought of actually working with an author. I would be working with someone that I had always admired. I am an avid reader. By that I mean, I read at least two to three books a week, sometimes more, if I have time. Authors are people that I put up on pedestals. People I envied and thought of very highly. How could someone like me, even begin to converse with such famous people, much less record and produce an audiobook they would like. Well, I soon realized that authors are just like you and me. They are everyday people, but people who have a special talent. The talent for putting words on a page to tell a story or relay an idea. And what was so neat, was that I was chosen to make their words leap from that page and come to life through sound. I would be able to share their story with others through the world of audio.

I want to tell you not a little, but a great deal about one of these authors. Her name is Sarah Walker

Gorrell. I would like to share with you the comments Sarah had put on the "about this title page" of her titles posting, for a narrator, for "Tales from the Porch". I am quoting Sarah, because I could not say it any better. <u>Comments from the Rights Holder:</u> *The majority of the short stories in 'Tales from the Porch' are upbeat and humorous and all are personal experiences, in one way or another. There are a couple of exceptions to the "upbeat, humorous" category - one being my "Letter to Bob," my husband who passed away as a result of Multiple Myeloma. While I'm traveling and seeing different sights, people, etc.,*

*I'm often creating stories in my head.
I view most of life as a story, and I
love to write about personal
experiences.*

*I am a mother, grandmother and
great grandmother with two noisy
(rescue) Pomeranians. I live in
southern Mississippi in the same
county where I was born. I love my
porch where I can sit and watch the
traffic rushing down my country
road. I'm a lover of black-eyed peas,
fried okra, cornbread, sweet tea and
people....and life and I'm really a
southern woman.*

*I have a blog titled 'from the front
porch' and have also written a
column, of the same name, for my*

local weekly newspaper. I am the Organist for my Methodist Church where my great-grandfather was one of the first pastors and where my maternal grandparents were married in 1910. I tell folks that "God sits with me on that Organ bench, and if you hear a sour note, that was Him!" I received a great review from Scott Hughes "Online Book Club" and have been very pleased that other reviews, on Amazon, have been good. I market my book on Twitter, my Facebook page, and any other online outlets available. My local Friends of the Library is sponsoring a Book Signing on April 24th.

When I read Sarah's comments, I knew immediately that I wanted to narrate and produce her audiobook. We are both Southern. We are both Grandmothers. We both love cornbread, black-eyed peas, and fried okra. There was nothing more that I wanted, at that particular time, than to be chosen to narrate and produce Sarah's audiobook. And even more so, when I read the audition script. It was so great. I submitted the audition that very day, April 28th. Then I sat back and waited, and waited, and waited. I started to get worried, although I knew that Sarah would probably be inundated with hundreds of narrators wanting to produce her audiobook, so she would have a huge amount of auditions to sort through. I kept checking ACX and noticed that the title was still accepting auditions, so I kept waiting, all the time trying not to expect to be chosen. I did not want to be devastated if my audition was rejected, so I did not get my expectations up too high. But, I did a lot of praying. I finally got an email on May 3 that Sarah had selected me to narrate and produce her audiobook. Needless to say, I was ecstatic. When I received and read the full Manuscript, I was even more thrilled. There are 73 short stories in Sarah's book. All life experiences. I laughed with the majority and cried with the others. I want to share one of those stories with you, a little teaser, of what is to come. I love this story. I can relate, since Sarah and I are close to the same age, and I know many of you will relate also. Be prepared, you will laugh so hard, it will bring you to tears.

A VISION IN MY OWN MIND
"To alleviate the boredom of the hotel room, during my many years as a "Road Warrior," trips to the nearest mall would often take place. On one of those shopping expeditions, as I was leaving the dressing room, I

noticed some appropriately placed packages of 'Spanx'. Spanx is a spandex girdle, designed to make you think it will put everything back where it is supposed to be. This was marketing at its best. Unless one is built like a model, we all need a little help to corral all those extra rolls of fat that somehow attach themselves to inappropriate places on our bodies – especially as one ages. I had just finished trying on two or three outfits. One of the outfits I had chosen was a pair of slacks along with a long tunic type sweater – one that would go practically to my thighs and cover up what I call the "wave effect". I am sure that you have seen the wave – it is when the tummy and thighs have those rolls of fat like the waves on the ocean. So, here I was, just the perfect victim for their sales gimmick. YES, I wanted those Spanx – they would certainly get rid of my waves. (Now, don't you think the term "waves" sound so much better than fat or flab?) I stood there, looking at the size chart on the package, trying to decide the best fit for me. I was at the top of the Size C; but vanity, ego, or just plain stupidity – call it whatever you will, would not let me look at Size D. After all, I once was a Size 8 and I was now on Weight Watchers; why buy a size that was going to be too big after just a few

more points! I grabbed my Size C
Spanx and headed for the cashier,
not only was I going to be well-
dressed, but I was also going to look
very svelte with everything in place. I
could just see an image of myself in
my head – all slim and trim (and it
only took one trip to the store to have
this vision swirling around in this old
brain). I was so excited, I could
hardly wait for morning! I pulled the
Spanx out of the package and
unfolded this tiny piece of spandex. I
held it up to my body and saw that
this was going to be one tight fit! I
briefly considered waiting for those
Weight Watcher points to take effect.
I sat down on the side of the hotel

bed, brought my right leg up and crossed it up over my left knee to make it easier to put on the darned things. As I was getting ready to pull the right leg of the Spanx over my right foot, I noticed a defect. There, in the crotch, was a hole! Upon closer inspection, I could see that this wasn't a tear – the hole had been left there, on purpose. I got up off the bed and dug the package out of the trash can. I had my own suspicions of why the opening was there, but I needed to read it for myself. There, on the back of the package, the benefits of my Spanx were listed. Included was "Slit in crotch for when necessity calls". Now, hadn't they just thought of everything! I could even be trim while I "pottied." It's just such a shame that the visions in our heads aren't the ones that look back at us when we stare in the mirror. I had not yet gotten them on, but I knew in my heart of hearts that putting this wonderful garment on was going to be no walk in the park! I sat back down on the side of the bed, and once again, I crossed the right leg and foot over the left knee. And, I started. I got the Spanx onto the right foot and up on my ankle. I put my foot down and leaned over and got the Spanx over the left foot and onto the ankle. I pulled and tugged and tugged and pulled until I had them up to my thighs. I continued pulling and tugging. I sat on the bed, and I lay on the bed - sweatin' like a pig. I waddled over and looked in the mirror. How in the world was I ever going to get them up over my butt, and where would all those lumps go? It looked to me like there was a lot more of me left than there was of Spanx. I began to rethink that size thing. After dancing around the room for several more minutes; losing a fake fingernail in the process, I won the battle. I was absolutely worn out, and every inch of me was drenched, in sweat. But, I was completely dressed, in Spanx, from my knees to my waist. There was only one small problem. I had managed to put the Spanx on over a pair of underwear and a pair of pantyhose. (Just like a man would do, I had read the instructions AFTER I started putting them on.)! Either I would ignore necessity calling, all day, or I would remove these things and start again. About that time, necessity did call – loud and clear. I decided, since I had to remove them anyway, I might as well put them on like they were designed to be worn, with pantyhose on top. Let me tell you, putting those things on a second time was no picnic. The first time was bad enough, but trying to pull Spanx onto bare, damp (from sweating) skin was like trying to put a 4-inch square peg into a 3-inch round hole! I struggled and pulled and twisted and danced around that room like I was having some sort of fit. Finally, after about 15 minutes and a couple of hot flashes, I was once again wrapped in Spanx. To say they fit like a glove was an understatement I looked in the mirror, and I must tell you that the sight just made me sick. I still had waves in all the wrong places. I had believed everything in the ads. I had really imagined that this wonderful garment would absolutely and miraculously get rid of all my lumps and ridges. Their ads had truly made me believe in magic. In my mind, I could see myself looking like I had 20 – 30 years ago. Not! The mind does really strange things. I could still imagine those new pants and that new tunic top making me look all slim and sexy. After all, I had the Spanx on – the image, in my head, would surely appear (in the mirror) when I was fully dressed. Let's just say the image in my head looked better than the one that stared back at me after I had on those new duds. To say that I was disappointed was putting it mildly. I suffered through the day. You just can't stuff a Size 14 body into a garment meant for a Size 8 and not expect discomfort. And, as for the "hole for when necessity called"

– well, that didn't work like it was supposed to, either. The darned things were just about as hard to get off as they were to get on. But, I tell you one thing – there is one place where they fit very well.......in my dresser drawer. I hang onto them for times when I need to look like a model. Do I put them on? Heck no, I open the drawer and look at 'em! The image in my head is quite enough."

Sarah Walker Gorrell

Sarah is a best-selling author. Her first endeavor at writing a novel was when she was invited by author, Mary Cooke who writes as Mary Lou Cheatham, to co-author "Travelers in Painted Wagons on Cohay Creek".

Sarah is currently working on "Built on Evil Ground" which she considers "factual fiction" about her grandfather, peonage, the Mississippi Delta, and the place where she now lives.

While working on Sarah's book, we have been in touch often, both by phone and through email. She always responds quickly if I have any questions. Sarah is a lovely person. She is funny, warm, and always seems to be upbeat. She kindly sent me an autographed copy of the paperback edition of "Tales from the Porch". She even sent me a friend request on Facebook and I follow her postings daily. Reading Sarah's postings on Facebook keeps me in stitches half of the time. I also read her blog. She is very genuine and very down to earth. I don't know why I was ever nervous about having contact with an author. If they are all like Sarah Walker Gorrell, I won't mind working with any of them.

My narration and production portion of the audiobook is completed. I received Sarah's final approval and now the book is with the ACX Quality Assurance Team. Hopefully, by the time this eBook is published, the audiobook will be on sale at Amazon, Audible.com. and iTunes. This has been a wonderful experience. I am not only part of an exceptional book. But have also made a life-long friend. You can purchase a print or Kindle copy of Sarah's book "Tales from the Porch' from Amazon. Keep an eye out for the audiobook. You can email me at laurajohnson.narrator@gmail.com and I will notify you when the audiobook goes on sale.

The one last thing I would like to tell you about is me and my life. I think it is important for you as the reader, to know something about, me, the narrator/producer and now, new author. I was born and raised in Texas. I moved to Florida at the age of sixteen, with my Mother, after she divorced my Father. There I remained for most of my life. I have one sibling, a brother, who was in the Navy for twenty-eight years and did two tours of Vietnam. He then became a Deputy Sheriff and now Is retired and lives in Alexandria, Virginia with his wife, who he met in London, while in the Navy. I was married and divorced twice and have one very handsome son, who has six very adorable children. Four of whom live with us.

I had no prior experience doing voice overs or acting before becoming an audiobook narrator. I was, however, an entertainer for more than thirty years of my adult life. I traveled on the road with a band, up and down the East Coast of the United States, from Florida to Maine. We were a dinner and dance band, playing jazz, rock and roll, country, easy listening, big band, etc. Our repertoire was extensive, which made us quite popular with the dinner clubs. I was the lead vocalist and front person for the trio. We had an absolute blast and met a lot of interesting people.

Now this was back in the 80's. Music was quite different then and live bands were widely sought after. And yes, I still spent a lot of my spare time reading. I may not have had experience before I became a narrator, but, yet, in a way, I did. The difference being, I told stories though my singing. Every time I sang a song, I was telling a story. Song writers are some the greatest story tellers there are. Through my music, people would laugh or sometimes cry, just like you do when reading a story in a book. So, in a way, I am doing the same thing now, that I did all those years ago. And I love it almost as much.

Today, I am a 69-year-old Mother and Grandmother. As I mentioned earlier in the book, I live with my son and four grandchildren, who I take care of and Homeschool. Since discovering and taking the *5 - Day Audiobook Audition Challenge* course from Krystal Wascher, I no longer search for a "work at home" job. I have finally found one that I am good at, and I am able to make money, while enjoying doing it. This is a profession and a career, not just a job. I look forward to recording every day. And every day, I look to see what new titles are posted that need narrators and producers. I am happy, confident, and wake up looking forward to what the new day will bring.

I have found that I love narrating books. I am fairly picky as to the books I choose to narrate. Because I am not comfortable creating different character voices, I pretty much stick to Nonfiction books. I totally cannot do different dialects, so I stay with General American and Southern American accents. The book I am narrating now is a fiction short story. It does have a couple of different characters, but I am only having to narrate the book as a story teller. I normally would not have chosen the book, but the author chose me. It is a book I did not audition for and I felt excited that I was asked to narrate it. They approved the first fifteen minutes, so my voice and style is what they are looking for. I will not be as hesitant to audition for this type of book in the future.

OK. You are about probably now wondering, what is the point here? Why am I reading this eBook? What can I get out of it? Well, I am hoping that telling you how I stumbled into the world of audiobook narration will ease the fears and pave the way for anyone who is on the fence, wondering if they can do this. Or for anyone looking for a "work at home job", that is fun and fulfilling. Or for anyone that loves to read and wants to learn how to share that love of reading with others through the wonderful world of audiobook narration. YOU CAN DO THIS!

Being an audiobook narrator is not a "get rich quick scheme". But, it is a very fulfilling and rewarding career. You can do this full time or in your spare time. At first, I thought, OK, maybe I will try for one audiobook a month. Well, now that I have experienced what it is narrate and produce audiobooks, I am hooked. I will gladly take on as many as my time will allow.

This is not rocket science. And it may not be a breeze to do in the beginning. I admit that with my very first audiobook, I struggled somewhat. I was not sure if I had the microphone too close to my mouth or too far away. I could not figure out how to hold the microphone and the pages of the manuscript at the same time. You see, when I started, I did not have a microphone stand or a paper holder, so I had to wing it. I had forgotten everything I learned in class about editing, so I had to review all the videos again. I was literally a mess with the first book. But I got encouragement from my family and from Krystal. I calmed myself down. I figured out what to do with the manuscript and the microphone, and I figured out how to proceed with the editing and mastering, and to perfect the final recording for export to an MP3 file.

So, don't listen to anyone that says you can't do this. If you love to read. If you read stories to your children or grandchildren, or anyone, then turn that love of reading, into a whole new world. Share that love of reading with others through audiobook narration. You may not become a millionaire, but I cannot express in words, what it is like to go on Amazon and see the words, "narrated by Laura Johnson", by the title of the audiobook that I narrated and produced. It is such a sense of accomplishment. And it just feels darn good.

I know, I know, you are thinking that I have not told you specifically, the details of how to become a narrator. What to do. The steps to take. I have gone into as much detail as I can, to peak your interest, and hopefully get you to take the steps necessary to check out Krystal's website and take the plunge. You won't be sorry you did. If you love to read and want to share that love of reading with others, while making money doing it, then Audiobook Narration could be the career for you. Go to Krystal Wascher's website for more information on audiobook narrator courses:

https://krystalwascher.com/ You can email me with any questions or if you just need help and support at:

laurajohnson.narrator@gmail.com

Thank you for reading this eBook. I hope it has given you the encouragement to take that step into the world of audiobook narration. I have shared a number of different aspects of the audiobook world with you, so you would get a little taste of what is involved, from taking the course, setting up an account, submitting auditions, and narrating an audiobook. You will meet all kinds of people from all walks of life, and from all around the world. By meeting them, not face to face, but through audiobooks. You will correspond with the authors or rights holders through email, through ACX messaging, or by phone. The rights holder from my second audiobook lived in Japan, so I would be messaging her while she slept, and she would be responding back to me while I slept. This is such a wonderful opportunity to become a part of a really special group of talented artists from all walks of life and from all over the world. Just take that first step and sign up for Krystal's course. You have nothing to lose and you will be glad you did.

I would greatly appreciate if you would leave a review when you are finished. Let me know your thoughts and honest opinion. Honest feedback is important to every author. You, our readers, are what keep us writing, and we as authors, want to know what you liked or didn't like about our book. Was there enough information? Was there too much information? Was it easy to understand? Was it enjoyable to read? Would you read another one of our books? I hope so. I am keeping notes of new and interesting things I discover as I embark on this new journey. I want to be able to expand on what I have written and add to my learning experiences. I am working on setting up a blog to share the world of audiobooks with other authors, narrators, and anyone simply interested in this exciting field. I believe we can all learn from each other.

I hope you have enjoyed reading this book, enough to share it with others. But what I hope for the most is that I have helped some or all of you start on your path to a new and exciting career in the wonderful world of audiobook narration. If you are an author and want to increase your sales by turning your book into an audiobook, you can find a narrator at ACX, or you can narrate your own book. Or maybe you are someone like me, who has been searching for just that right fit and hearing about this field strikes a chord within you. Whoever you are and whatever your goals, this could be a life changing career for you. Thank you for reading my book. And best of luck in whatever career path you choose. I hope all of your dreams come true.